Note

Once a reader can recognize and identify the 20 words used to tell this story, he or she will be able to read successfully the entire book. These 20 words are repeated throughout the story, so that young readers will be able to easily recognize the words and understand their meaning.

The 20 words used in this book are:

at	monster	quick	the
door	monsters	seven	three
eight	more	shut	two
five	nine	six	where
four	one	ten	window

Library of Congress Cataloging-in-Publication Data

Namm, Diane.
    Monsters!/by Diane Namm: illustrated by Maxie Chambliss.
        p. cm — (My first reader)
        Summary: A little boy counts ten monsters in his room at bedtime but he is able to get rid of them all.
            ISBN 0-516-05358-2
            (1. Monsters — Fiction. 2. Counting. 3. Stories in rhyme.)
    I. Chambliss, Maxie, ill. II. Title. III. Series.
    PZ8.3. N27Mo   1990   90-30162
    (E) — dc20   CIP
                                                          AC

Monsters!

Monsters!

Written by Diane Namm   Illustrated by Maxie Chambliss

CHILDREN'S PRESS
 A Division of Grolier Publishing
Sherman Turnpike
Danbury, Connecticut 06816

Text © 1990 Nancy Hall, Inc. Illustrations © Maxie Chambliss.
All rights reserved. Published by Childrens Press®, Inc.
Printed in the United States of America. Published simultaneously in Canada.
Developed by Nancy Hall, Inc. Designed by Antler & Baldwin Design Group.

9 10 R 99

One monster

Two monsters

Three monsters

Four!

Where? At the window!

Where? At the door!

Five monsters

Six monsters

Seven monsters more!

Three at the window!

Four at the door!

Eight monsters

Nine monsters

Ten monsters more!

Quick, shut the window!

Quick, shut the door!